# GROWING
*Your*
# FAITH

SEEDS OF INSPIRATION SERIES
BOOK 1

# GROWING
## *Your*
# FAITH

## 25 DEVOTIONAL STORIES
## FOR WOMEN

# ROBYN DYKSTRA

Gossamer Press

ISBN: 978-1-7378180-0-7 Hardcover
ISBN: 978-1-7378180-1-4 Paperback
ISBN: 978-1-7378180-2-1 Ebook

Editor: Ginger Kolbaba
Copyeditor: Bob Hartig, The Copy Fox
Interior Design and Typesetting: Katherine Lloyd, The Desk
Cover Design: DesignART
Cover Art / Interior Art: Lavalove

# Contents

# A QUICK MESSAGE
# FROM ROBYN

*T*he devotional stories in *Growing Your Faith* come right out of real life. They are filled with words of encouragement to help you stay true to Jesus and true to yourself and not to worry about perfectionism and people pleasing. I pray you find yourself in the stories, nodding in agreement. Failing forward. Trying your best. Becoming more like Jesus.

I know you. And, friend, just like you, I'm a work in progress. I'd like you to think I'm superwoman, but just like you, I can't do it all, and occasionally I need to wear my cleanest dirty pair of underwear inside out because I just haven't gotten to the laundry. I've eaten lots of expired food because I'm too busy and distracted to read labels. Some days I miss opportunities because I'm simply too scared to try (again) and fail.

But here's the thing: I know I am loved, and I know that, in Jesus, I am enough. That's what I pray for you: to know you are all that and a bag of chips plus a brownie—loved and enough.

The devotional stories in *Growing Your Faith* were written for you. Laugh with me. Learn from me. Lean on me and let me lead you to Jesus.

When you get to the end of this little book, you'll inevitably want more stories like these. I'm writing as fast as I can, but in the meantime, go to www.robyndykstra.com/blog to get your fix.

# 1

# GOODNESS, GOD! WHAT ARE YOU UP TO?

I trust in you, LORD;

I say, "You are my God."

—PSALM 31:14

*I* know God is good and has good things in store for me. The Bible tells us over and over that he has good plans for us.

He's definitely given me great blessings and commissioned me to do good things:

He called me to be his own.

Hurrah!

He called me to be a wife.

Hurrah, hurrah!

He called me to be a mom.

Hip, hip, hurrah!

He called me into the workforce and then into full-time ministry as a speaker and author.

Booyah!

Such wonderful plans. And I have embraced those callings with alacrity and joy. But sometimes God's goodness and plans for me don't always look the way I think they should.

Instead of a wide-open road toward success, sometimes it seems more like I'm running into roadblocks and detours.

Have you had that experience? You know God has good plans for your life. You know he is calling you to do something special for him. *But* . . . you're finding more roadblocks than open roads.

That's when we have to remind ourselves of God's faithfulness. He asks us to trust him and to be faithful with his call on our lives.

Even when we don't understand what he's up to.

Even when we want to know more of the details.

Even when the outcome looks bleak.

In those moments when we question his goodness, his faithfulness, his trustworthiness, we can find strength in God's Word.

God called Noah to build an ark to escape the coming flood. But Noah had to wait and work and trust God for 120 years.

Abraham was promised an heir, but he got old waiting. He trusted God for twenty-five years before he got his son Isaac.

God gave Joseph a dream that he would one day be great, but then he was kidnapped, sold into slavery, falsely accused, and imprisoned! Even so, he trusted God for thirteen years before God raised him up to second in command of Egypt and saved his family from starvation.

David was called to be king. And he trusted God through battles and persecution for twenty-five years before taking the throne.

Mary was called to birth our Savior, Jesus. She trusted God through the gossip and the fear of being stoned.

Men and women in the center of God's will and calling were met with opposition, ridicule, torment, and anguish. But they didn't stop proclaiming God's goodness, and they didn't stop trusting him.

And neither should we.

*Trust him or fail him: those are the choices.*

We can trust him for the timing, the provision, and the protection until we see the fullness of his faithfulness.

Or we can quit on his calling. Circumvent his plan. Foil our future. Miss out on experiencing his pleasure.

David said, "I trust in you, LORD; I say, 'You are my God.'"

I choose to trust him. Even if it means repeating, "I trust you, God. I trust you, God. I trust you, God . . ." until the anxiety, worry, fear, or sorrow subsides.

A thousand times a day if necessary.

You may need to do that too.

When your baby goes off to kindergarten or college, you can say, "I trust you, God."

When you get the promotion or the pink slip . . . "I trust you, God."

When the diagnosis is benign or malignant . . . "I trust you, God."

When all is well or the well is dry . . . "I trust you, God."

Though we may not always know what God is up to, we can always trust his goodness and faithfulness toward us.

# Prayer

Though I am afraid and may falter,

God, be with me and assure

me of your goodness

so that I may trust you

all my days and

in all my ways. Amen.

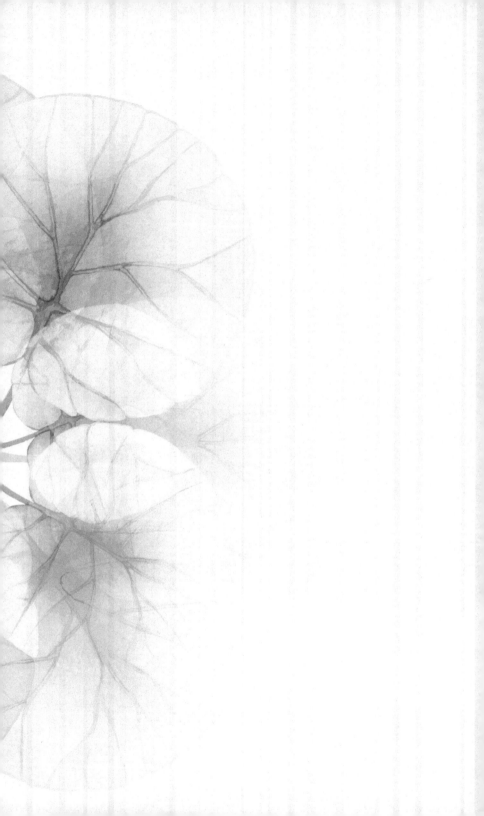

# 2

# WAITING FOR GOD'S GOOD GIFTS

Every good and perfect gift is from above,
coming down from the Father
of the heavenly lights, who does not
change like shifting shadows.

—JAMES 1:17

From the time my children were born, I planned to give them lots of gifts. I intended to shower them with opportunities that would delight them. I was determined to give them things that would make their lives easier or better or richer or set them up for success.

As far as it depended on me, they would swim in an ocean, ride a bike, drive a car, have a girlfriend, attend college, mow the lawn with the big tractor, use a chainsaw, manage money.

Even so, I knew I couldn't dump every good thing I had in my storehouse on them at once! I didn't want them to become overwhelmed or spoiled or entitled. I didn't want to set my boys up to fail or get hurt.

Did you notice that most of the grand gifts I had for them required training to appreciate and manage? I couldn't toss my infant into the ocean. Or give the car keys to a four-year-old. And they'd have to grow tall enough to reach the pedals on the tractor!

In order for my gifts to be a blessing and not a curse, I had to dispense my treasures to my boys as they exhibited the maturity to be blessed by them.

God has a storehouse full of riches and resources for you and me. Like any good parent, he longs to see his children supplied with gifts to walk in their calling, to be equipped and fulfilled for their work, and to be surrounded by people who will cheer them on. But he won't give us those gifts all at once! He measures them out to us based on our maturity and readiness.

How do we access that storehouse of treasures and gain maturity? Very simply, we pray!

We may ask for his blessings, but if he doesn't instantly grant our request, we must not get discouraged. While God is holding all sorts of good things for us, he won't give them to us until the right time. He won't set us up to fail or to be corrupted by the gifts he has for us.

But we want things *now*, don't we? We're accustomed to having what we want immediately. Overnight deliveries. Drive-through sustenance. Instant hot water. Immediate internet access.

When we pray for God to give us his good gifts, the desires of our hearts, and we don't receive them immediately, consider that the answer is yes, but maybe not yet.

Remember how God sent Moses to lead the Israelites out of slavery? It took Moses ten miraculous signs before they received their freedom (see Exodus 7–12). What if God was calling you to persevere through all ten plagues. Would you? Or would you bail at the third or the seventh or even the

ninth, thinking you must have heard wrong or that God changed his mind?

What about Joshua and the tribes of Israel whom God told to march around Jericho for seven days (see Joshua 6)? What if they had stopped marching after one day? Or after three days? Or after six?

If you were Joshua, would you have been able to withstand the grumbling and questioning from the masses? Would you have been able to press on and get the victory? Or would you have settled for the puny bit of land on the shores of the Red Sea?

Girlfriend, don't settle for less than all the gifts God has in his storehouse for you. I assure you that God is ready to partner with you to make your life better or richer or to set you up for success. Look at all the things you've already received. Count all the bonuses and benefits you have. He's not finished giving to you yet!

# Prayer

God, thank you that

I can trust you,

and that you are a good,

good Father who loves me.

Let me wait patiently for the

abundance, joy, and good gifts

you have promised to me.

Amen.

# 3

# MAKING ROOM
# FOR THE NEW

The LORD had said to Abram,
"Go from your country,
your people and your father's household to
the land I will show you. . . .
So Abram went,
as the LORD had told him.

—GENESIS 12:1, 4

*A*s I put the sewing box back in the closet, I spotted three big white cardboard boxes tucked so far back I had to crawl in to drag them out. Each of the dust-covered, shrink-wrapped boxes had a large plastic window that displayed a wedding dress bodice hermetically sealed inside.

The smallest box contained the wedding dress I wore to marry Jay (or Hot & Hunky, as I called him). It was a high-collared, lacy gown with long, poofy lace sleeves. Not the least bit sexy. I was trying to get his mother's approval since Jay married me just months after I quit my job as a Playboy Bunny. Fourteen years later, my heart broke and my world imploded when Jay died suddenly of a heart attack at thirty-nine years old.

The next box held an ivory satin sheath that flattered the flawless figure I'd earned from grieving Hot & Hunky. (When I'm sad, I don't eat.) Even at forty-one, I looked more like a model than a mom when I walked down the aisle to marry Craig, Adventure Boy.

A pilot error, a thunderstorm, and a mountain range created a trifecta of tragedy that took Adventure Boy's life at the age of forty-one.

The last box held the five-hundred-pound white-beaded gown I wore to marry Dave, Mr. 4-Ever, who is, I am happy to report, holding up remarkably well.

The decades have ticked off while those dresses sat in their plastic prisons. Even if I wanted to wear them again, I'd never get them zipped over my thicker, well-padded frame.

I treasured the memories but realized I didn't need those dresses to remind me of a special day. I no longer wanted them to fasten me emotionally to a previous time, man, or broken dream.

Out of fear I pretended was reverence, I had remained attached to what was good or purposeful once, but which no longer served my life. It was time to make room for something new. The wedding dresses could better serve elsewhere. So I gave them away.

One made its way to Costa Rica to make another bride's day special. Another was cut up to make a burial gown for a baby's funeral. One decorates a friend's barn that serves as a wedding venue.

Some things you keep because they serve you—a quilt your grandma made or a photo of your wedding day. Other things you get rid of to make room for something new that can move you unhindered into your future.

Just as Abram trusted God by packing up and moving on, we have to let go of the very good and familiar to find the land where God will bless us.

Just as Job, who endured great tribulation, moved past the trials to recreate a new life and family, we have to forgive and move on.

When Peter betrayed Jesus, his future could have been forfeit, but he allowed Jesus to restore him and let go of his failures, and we have to believe Jesus forgives us too.

What thing of the past needs to leave so you have room for the new thing God has for you?

Is God calling you into something new, as he did Abram? Have you passed through a trial you hold on to like it's an old friend? Is there a mistake in your past that still causes you shame, even though Jesus has offered restoration? Could today be the day you evaluate what's taking up the space in your mind and heart that God wants to fill with new thoughts and dreams?

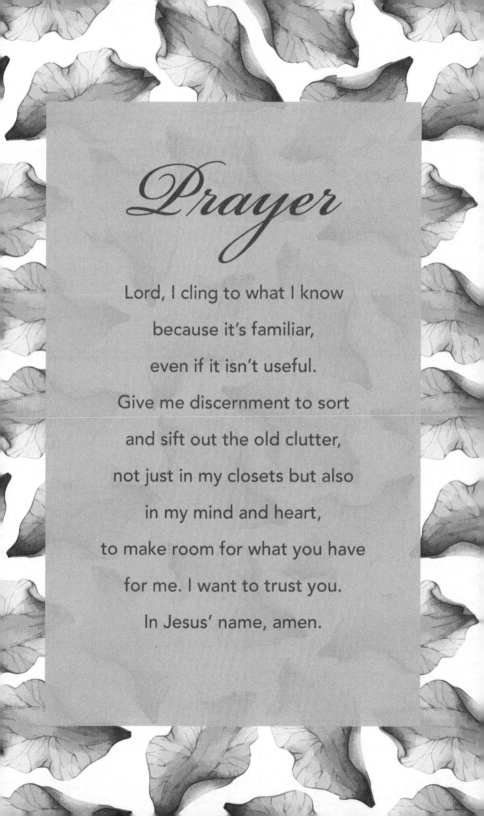

# Prayer

Lord, I cling to what I know

because it's familiar,

even if it isn't useful.

Give me discernment to sort

and sift out the old clutter,

not just in my closets but also

in my mind and heart,

to make room for what you have

for me. I want to trust you.

In Jesus' name, amen.

# 4

# DOES GOD ALLOW MORE THAN WE CAN HANDLE?

God is our refuge and strength,
an ever-present help in trouble.
Therefore we will not fear, though the
earth give way and the mountains fall into
the heart of the sea, though
its waters roar and foam and the
mountains quake with their surging.

—PSALM 46:1–3

*H*as anyone told you that God won't give you more than you can handle? I've heard that comment plenty. And there was a time when I believed it.

Then I buried two husbands and my mama in four years. God definitely allowed more than I could handle!

I'm sure you can relate. Haven't you had seasons when the kids were little and you got no sleep and thought you were losing your mind? Or when someone you loved was addicted or abusive, and you feared for your sanity or safety? Or when you experienced a time of lack, sickness, or upheaval that you thought would crush you?

Of course you have. And that's when God does his best work. It is in the times of upheaval that we run to him for the healing, rescue, answers, resolution, or miracle we desperately need . . . but which is so very far beyond our own control or ability to resolve.

If we could manage everything in our lives, why in the world would we need God?

In 1 Corinthians 10:13 (NRSV), the apostle Paul tells us, "No testing has overtaken you that is not common to everyone. God is faithful, and he will not let you be tested beyond your strength, but with the testing he will also provide the way out so that you may be able to endure it."

"God is faithful and will not let you be tested beyond your strength" sounds a lot like *God won't give you more than you can handle*. But we have to understand the context of the passage. Paul is not addressing tragic circumstances like death, disease, and imminent peril. He's telling his readers that it's possible to rule over the temptation of our former sinful and destructive practices.

We must not be deceived by those who would ask us to endure our hardships on our own—or all alone.

Before I had my come-to-Jesus moment, I tried to manage life on my own and failed miserably. I let my circumstances dictate my emotional state. If "things" weren't going well, I wasn't well. I had meltdowns and threw temper tantrums rivaling Rumpelstiltskin. That's no way to manage anything!

Or I'd disengage and sink into a puddle of discouragement, believing that all was lost so I might as well eat, drink, and be merry on my way to die.

We just can't fall for the lie that God won't give us more than we can handle. While no one would desire the loss, sickness, or hardships that drive us to beg God for help, those are the seasons we can experience the greatest intimacy with God. It's in the times of desperately crying out to him that we tend to be most in tune with his voice and open to his leading.

When you are out of your mind, or over your head, or under attack, don't try to manage it on your own. Call on God, who is for you and will be with you through it all. He will give you the strength you need to press on. He will provide the support you need to persevere. He will lead you to the solutions you need to survive.

When life reels out of control, don't try to brave it alone. Run to God.

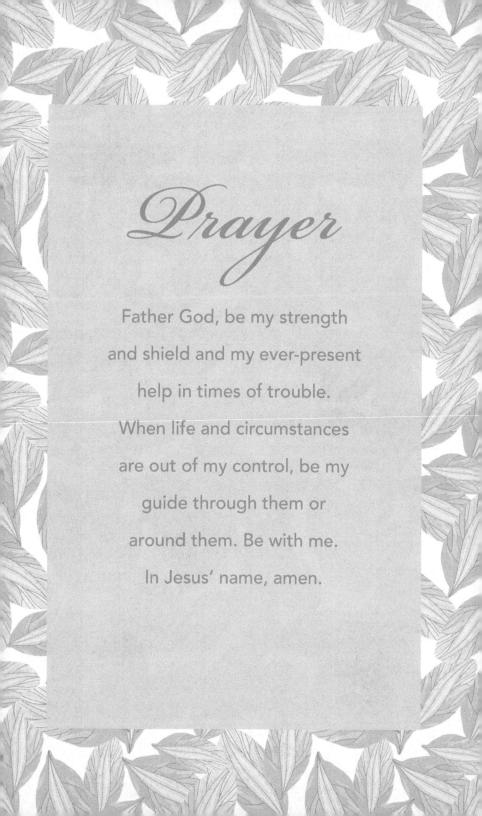

# *Prayer*

Father God, be my strength
and shield and my ever-present
help in times of trouble.
When life and circumstances
are out of my control, be my
guide through them or
around them. Be with me.
In Jesus' name, amen.

# 5

# ENTERING A DREADED
# NEW SEASON

Remember not the former things,

nor consider the things of old.

Behold, I am doing a new thing;

now it springs forth,

do you not perceive it?

—ISAIAH 43:18–19 ESV

*U*h oh!

I felt like Dorothy in *The Wizard of Oz* the Tuesday morning I heard the tornado alarms broadcasting on the radio. A lulu of a storm was picking up strength, speed, and lots of water as it made its way across Lake Michigan toward my house.

I immediately started praying for God's protection. As I reached for my Bible to read from Psalms, I remembered I'd left it at church the night before, since I was supposed to be back there this morning to lead a Bible study. Wow, had that been a bad idea! Decades of sermon notes, lecture prompts, and favorite passages were written in the margins and highlighted for reference, and now it was at risk of being destroyed. I had to rescue that Bible!

The weatherman's announcement was urgent: "Take cover. The storm is due to hit our area in twenty-seven minutes!"

I calculated the drive time and decided to make a run for it. Rain pelted the windshield as I drove through the neighborhood and into the church parking lot. I kept watch on the darkening sky as I fumbled for the keys to the church. Once inside, I ran to the classroom where I taught several sessions of Bible study every week, grabbed my Bible, and tore back home, arriving just in time to get to the basement with "My Precious" for company. Hot tears of relief rolled down my face as I hugged the fat book with the busted-up cover.

Some may think putting myself in danger that way was foolish. But that Bible had kept me company for decades of Sunday services and comforted me through the deaths of two husbands and countless smaller trials. It dispensed wisdom during the long years of parenting alone and pointed me to my Savior in times of despair and moments of temptation. God made himself known to me in its pages.

I clung to my Bible and waited out the storm. We were safe!

We'd been through so much together. I was devastated when recently I noticed the small print in my tattered volume becoming increasingly difficult to read. I held on as long as I could, but I knew I needed a new Bible. Reluctantly, I invested in a super-giant-print one.

I took my new purchase home and ran my fingers along the smooth edges. Pretty as it was, I didn't appreciate its clean pages and empty margins. In theory, I knew this new Bible would make my study time more enjoyable and easier on the eyes, but the truth was that I missed the familiarity of my old Bible with its notes and scribbles and tear-stained pages.

I was entering a new season and I wasn't ready to.

Have you ever been forced into a new season? Maybe you've experienced a job change, or your BFF moved away. Perhaps your doctor retired (the nerve!), or your beloved pet died, and you are feeling the loss as you navigate the unfamiliar without the benefit of your faithful comforter.

The good news about facing these seasons is that God is in the business of renewal. Sometimes he has to move the old stuff out of the way so we are open to the new. That was my experience. I began to focus on what fresh insights I could discover as I used this new Bible. So I opened to the dedication page and I filled in the blanks:

**Presented to**

Begin a new era without fear

**By**

trusting and obeying God

**On**

all matters

What new thing is God doing in your life or asking you to let go of?

# Prayer

God, change is hard.

I cling to the old things that I know,

the things that bring comfort even

when you have something better for

me. Lord, lead me to the best for my

life. I know I can trust you

to deliver the good stuff because you

didn't hold back your

only Son from me.

In Jesus' name, amen.

# 6

# THE TOUGH STUFF
# OF PRUNING

[Jesus said,] "I am the true vine,
and my Father is the gardener.
He cuts off every branch in me that bears
no fruit, while every branch
that does bear fruit he prunes so that
it will be even more fruitful."

—JOHN 15:1–2

*T*he older I get, the furrier I become! I'm not even talking about my legs or armpits or places seen only by Mr. 4-Ever. I'm talking about the dark, thick hairs on my upper lip, the tufts growing out of my nostrils, and the whiskers jutting out of my chin! My natural eyebrow arch has morphed into a dash. Hair is growing up my forehead and under my brows like ivy on a brick wall.

So one day, as I was driving past a hairstyling shop by my house, I noticed a sign in the window that announced, "HAIR THREADING." Unlike the open-air chairs at the mall, this place afforded privacy.

Now, if you have never been threaded, let me explain the process. A technician puts you in a chair that reclines under lights as bright as the sun. She quickly assesses your face as she shakes her head in pity and disbelief that you have had to walk around in public with this horrible growth.

"Oh, honey! You should have come in sooner. You want your whole face done?"

"No, just my brows today."

"Oh, honey, you sure?" she says with a look of disgust as she hands me the 10x-magnifying glass that reveals *every single hair* on my face.

"Mmm, just the brows today."

"Okay," she says sorrowfully and gets to work. She unrolls a long piece of white thread from an enormous spool and winds it around her fingers like an elaborate game of cat's cradle. As I hold my skin taut, she traps the hair in the twisted threads and pulls.

Oh. My. Yikes. It hurts!

My eyes start to water. I sneeze. My nose runs. She hands me a tissue. *Why am I paying this woman to torture me?* More tears. More sneezing. More pauses to dab at my nose and eyes.

Eighteen tissues later, I am released from the torture chair and given the 10x-magnifying mirror. I'm ecstatic. I look like a movie star! Well, at least my eyebrows do.

As I pay the bill, she asks if I want to book my next appointment.

"Absolutely!" I say.

I needed that pruning. Even more so, though, I need the kind of pruning that only God provides as he shapes me into becoming more like Jesus.

Jesus told us that he is the vine and we are the branches. Every branch is under scrutiny. For our own good, for the good of others, and to glorify the Father, God either cuts off or prunes every branch. While pruning is painful, it exposes unhealthy branches and provides space for new growth. Pruning is ultimately for our good.

Consider my friend Jackie's situation. After being let go from a well-paying job, she was forced to find new employment. Though the initial experience was painful, she eventually found work that paid more, had a better environment, and wonderful coworkers.

Or consider Karen, who sold the home she raised her family in so she could move across country to care for her elderly mom. While purging and packing the house, a tangible sense of satisfaction and freedom fell on her, knowing she wouldn't be saddling her kids with a big mess.

Although painful, Rhea had to extricate herself from a long-term friendship. Though she'd begun to feel trapped and exhausted, she wanted to be a spiritual light in her friend's darkness. Finally God showed Rhea that she could pray for her friend and wish her well without remaining close.

Pruning is definitely unpleasant, but if we trust the One who's doing the pruning, we will always reap a benefit.

# Prayer

God, I know I need to be

constantly prepared for change

and pruning to experience

all the growth and joy you

intend for me. Give me grace

and courage to face these times,

trusting you have my best in mind.

In Jesus' name, amen.

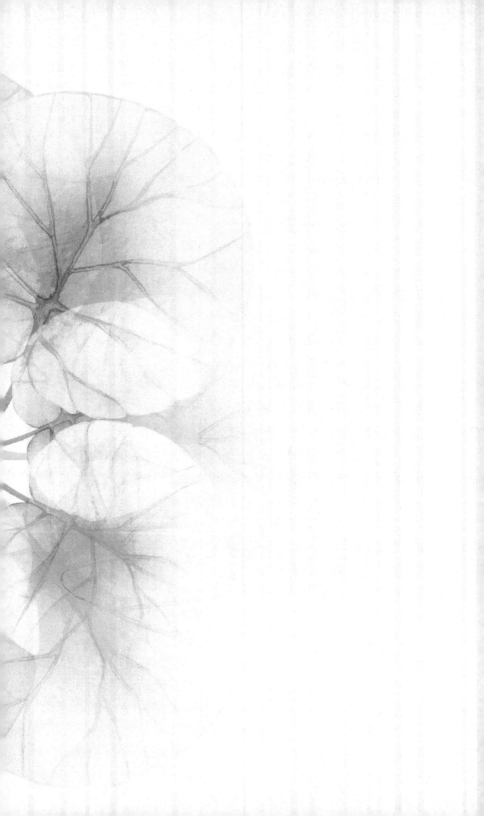

# 7

# THE BIG PICTURE

Let your light shine before others,
that they may see your good deeds
and glorify your Father in heaven.

—MATTHEW 5:16

*A*fter decades of feeding family and friends, several temporary live-ins, and many welcome—though often unexpected—guests, I can assure you that I am an expert grocery shopper.

I've planned more meals than I can count, written thousands of lists, and taken zillions of trips to the store. Since I lean more toward utilitarian work than decorative, I never make one of anything I cook. Though the pots are bigger, it's really not any more difficult to make two, three, or dare I say six times the recipe. This method gives me the liberty to offer hospitality spontaneously and provide emergency meals generously.

As with any good service, it's easy to slip into feeling good about doing the work instead of experiencing the pleasure of the One I serve. This especially becomes noticeable at the grocery store—where my compassion can easily morph into competition.

I compete to get a great parking spot, save money, collect all my items quickly, and expedite my checkout. I go to great lengths to win this private competition! I base my meal plan on the weekly store sales advertisement. I prepare my shopping list according to the product layout at the store. I hum along, zipping my cart around old men and new moms like a race car driver. And at the checkout, I scan the lanes for cashiers I know who are fast and who will pack my groceries like an engineer. When I find a promising line, I look to see who's ahead of me.

Based on their technique of unloading their cart, I determine if they are proficient or novices before getting behind them.

It never fails, though, that when I go into competitive mode, God steers me back toward compassion. When the deli counter clerk is serving number 12, I get number 2078 so I can chat with fellow shoppers. Or I'm forced to smile warmly at the lady blocking my aisle as she deliberates slowly between Metamucil and Benefiber. God prompts me to compliment frazzled employees and engage in conversation with friendly workers.

Though at first I didn't appreciate his interventions, the investment in compassion has become its own reward. I experience a fellow human's smile. I watch the face of a dejected employee light up. I make the day of a lonely fellow customer. And with a kind word, I witness the change in attitude of a cross worker.

Compassion for others is God's golden opportunity for you and me to make someone's day. To bring value to someone's life with a word or a smile. To say to a fellow, "You matter."

And yesterday, God rewarded me with a gesture of compassion, or "favorball," as we call it at our house. After years of idle conversation, random smiles, and patiently waiting my turn in line, I found myself late for an appointment and fifth in line at the checkout, behind fully loaded carts belonging to customers who had obviously not been in a grocery store since the digital age began.

When I felt my irritation rise, I took a deep breath and exhaled a private prayer. *God, let me be a representation of you to the world waiting to know you.*

Just as I finished, I felt a tap on my shoulder. One of the favorite cashiers was calling me to an open lane. I sailed through her lane and made it to my appointment with time to spare.

No competition.

God's way every time.

Win, Win.

The next time you find yourself feeling less than compassionate, take a moment to consider the bigger, more important, picture of what God wants you to be to a world who needs to know Jesus.

# *Prayer*

God,

let me find the reserve

in you to be who

you would be

in every situation.

Amen.

# 8

# ARE YOU IN
# THE CRAZY TREE?

Our Father in heaven,

hallowed be your name.

Your kingdom come, your will be done,

on earth as it is in heaven.

—MATTHEW 6:9–10 ESV

*T*he crazy tree is the one you climb when life is out of control. When people you love don't behave properly, or money is way short, or you discover a secret that you wish you hadn't.

I'm a big advocate of doing life in a community where your BFF can see you climbing the crazy tree from her kitchen window and holler at you to come down and have coffee.

But sometimes you're too quick, too sneaky, and you get past her. Then you find yourself in the crazy tree alone and scared, where the self-talk is all negative. It's bad, and you don't know how to get back down, and you can feel yourself melting down. When that happens, you have to perform CPR on yourself: Crisis Prayer Request.

In moments of crazy or fear or worry or calamity, when the enemy is whispering to give up, the *only* thing that will help is for *heaven to invade earth.* You need a spotlight of God's faithfulness and love to rescue you, to permeate your circumstances so you can release the crazy and climb out of that tree. Here's how CPR works:

First, focus on God, not on the crazy. Say God's names out loud: *God, you are my Father. Savior. Redeemer. King. Shield. Rock. Creator. Deliverer.* This is who he is.

Then declare God's attributes out loud. Remind yourself and your circumstances and any spiritual enemy

46

within listening range of all the character attributes of God you can think of: *God, you are faithful. Benevolent. Strong. Loving. Awesome. Fierce. Patient. Holy. You are for me.*

Focusing on who God is and what he does will reframe your mind so you can be thankful of the ways he works in and through your life. Thank God for all the blessings he's bestowed on you already: *Thank you, God, for my health. This home. My family of origin. The clean water that flows freely from my faucets. The electricity that runs my appliances. The food that tastes so good. The rivers of asphalt to drive on and my climate-controlled car for my comfort.*

When you have stood firm declaring God's character and God's attributes and you have sincerely thanked him for what you already have, then it's time to be still and listen.

That's right, be still and listen for God's reply or instruction or assurance. You may have a thought that traipses across the backyard of your brain. A song or a picture may come to mind. A name or Scripture may bubble to the surface of your memory. God speaks to us in many ways, but speak to us he does.

Next time you're in the crazy tree, practice praising,

reminiscing, thanking, and being still. When you call on God to bring heaven to earth, he does just that. God turns your crazy to calm so you can climb down out of the tree. Test him in this. When you call out to God, he hears you and recognizes your voice. God will respond to your call. You can trust him in this.

# Prayer

God, I am your child. As my Father
and Creator, I beg you to make yourself
known to me. Invade my crazy with
your calm. Your word says you
are near. You tell me not be anxious
about anything, but in every situation,
by prayer and petition,
with thanksgiving, to present my
requests to you so that your peace,
which transcends all understanding,
will guard my heart and mind
in Christ Jesus. Keep your word and
bring heaven to earth so I can
climb out of the crazy tree.
Replace my panic with your peace.
In Jesus' name, amen.

# 9

# WHAT'S THAT STINK?

These are written that you may
believe that Jesus is the Messiah,
the Son of God, and that by believing you
may have life in his name.

—JOHN 20:31

*W*hat do you do when the washing machine over-flows? How do you react to a really negative post on your Facebook page? Can you keep your cool when your curling iron overheats and melts your hair? Imagine discovering that your car has been towed!

Delays, disappointments, and doubts stink! And at some point, we all have to face the stinky stuff in our lives.

In John 11, Lazarus was deathly sick, and his sisters, Mary and Martha, were stuck in a stinky situation. They sent for Jesus, and when Jesus finally showed up, Lazarus had already died and been in the grave four days!

The sisters were crying, the mourners were crying, even Jesus cried. As they stood weeping and wailing at the cave/grave where a stone sealed in the body of Lazarus, Jesus made the most remarkable request: "Take away the stone."

"But Lord," Martha said, "by now there is a bad odor!"

"Did I not tell you that if you believe, you will see the glory of God?" Jesus told her.

When faced with a big stink, it's easier to leave well enough alone. To settle for what you've got instead of con-tending for all the good stuff God has for you.

At Jesus' request, they obeyed and took away the stone—and there was a stink!

The stink wasn't there to symbolize sin. Nothing in the text indicates Lazarus was struck down because of sin. The stink was there . . . to *delay* God's glory from being revealed, to *distract* them from seeing the miraculous, and to *detour* them in doubt instead of believing.

They had to *push through* the stink to get the miracle.

The same is true for us. Sometimes we have to push through the stink to get to the good stuff. But, friend, good stuff is coming!

After they rolled away the stone, Jesus called in a loud voice, "Lazarus, come out!" And the dead man walked out!

I don't know what kind of stink you may be facing today, but if the Holy Spirit is telling you to do, or to go, or to say something that seems wild and outlandish, just do it. Face down your fears, push through the stink, and claim your miracle or your calling or your peace.

Don't let stink *delay* God's glory from being revealed in your life. Decide not to let stink *distract* you from seeing the miraculous. Above all, don't let stink *detour* you into doubt instead of believing.

It takes courage and perseverance to push through the stink that's distracting or detouring you. It's hard to kick that addiction, forgive someone who's hurt you or betrayed you, pray fervently for a prodigal, stay invested in a difficult marriage, keep your job, quit your job, or start a job. But you can be assured that a fresh testimony waits for you just beyond the stink.

# Prayer

Jesus, thank you for

drawing me to yourself.

Use my story, my mess,

my moments to reveal

yourself to others.

Amen.

# 10

# PAINFUL AND AWKWARD CONFESSIONS

Jesus said to his disciples,
"Whoever wants to be my disciple
must deny themselves and take up
their cross and follow me."

—MATTHEW 16:24

*M*y son and I were at the Krispy Kreme drive-through, coupon in hand. We were moments away from warm, frosted doughnuts, but something was wrong with the coupon I was trying to use. I wanted chocolate frosted but the coupon was for glazed. I put up quite a fuss to get my discount and finally succeeded.

Pulling away victorious, doughnuts in hand, my boy looked at me and said, "Mom, you were really mean to that lady."

Ugh! Caught! As I quickly did a mental rewind, I knew he was right.

"Son, I was. Will you forgive me for talking to her like that?"

"Sure, Mama. Can I have a doughnut?"

As he ate his circle of deliciousness, I silently asked God to forgive me for modeling behavior I would never tolerate from the young man sitting next to me. I thought that was done, but the Holy Spirit laid his hand on my heart, prompting me to return and apologize to the girl at Krispy Kreme.

With the store already disappearing in my rearview mirror and using the traffic zipping by at breakneck speeds, I justified why I couldn't go back.

The Holy Spirit wasn't having any of it. For three days, he kept the pressure on until I couldn't stand it anymore.

Back at Krispy Kreme, I asked for Rose. She came from her position at the drive-through window to greet me at the counter.

"Hi," I said as friendly as I could. "You waited on me at

the drive-through three days ago, and I was very rude to you. I came to say I was sorry."

She looked at me for a split second. "I don't remember you."

"Well, I remember you," I said, taken aback but committed to making amends. "And I have come back to apologize."

"Okay, is that all you need from me?" she said.

Now I felt really awkward. "Well, yes, I am sorry. I shouldn't have talked to you like that. Will you forgive me?"

"It doesn't matter."

"It *does* matter! My God loves you too much to let me talk to you that way."

I would love to tell you that God broke through, and she cried, and I cried, and she surrendered her life to Jesus, but that isn't what happened. She looked at me as if I were an alien, then said with an attitude of indifference, "Whatever!" Then she turned on her heel and went back to her position at the window, leaving me standing there stunned.

*What in the world? God, why would you drag me back here to be humiliated and embarrassed if you weren't going to use this for your glory?*

But then I realized. My apologizing wasn't necessarily about Rose or her salvation. While I hopefully planted a seed on her journey of faith, the action was about me learning to keep a clean slate with God. And because we represent him to others: "We are therefore Christ's ambassadors, as though God were making his appeal through us" (2 Corinthians 5:20).

When the Holy Spirit nudges you to make things right, and you do, and you don't get the result you expect, take heart. You're getting a better result. A result that is making you more like Jesus. So the next time you feel the Holy Spirit nudge you, don't wait. Humble yourself and be obedient. You'll become a great disciple and a really good ambassador.

# Prayer

Father, give me

the courage to do

what you ask of me

for my own good

and your glory.

In Jesus' name, amen.

# 11

# FASTING FROM TELEVISION

Whatever is true, whatever is noble,
whatever is right, whatever is pure,
whatever is lovely, whatever is
admirable—if anything is excellent
or praiseworthy—think about
such things.

—PHILIPPIANS 4:8

*I* decided to fast from television for a while so I could connect with God in a personal way and consider what Christ's gift of salvation really means. Much of the Christian world gives up something during Lent. But Lent isn't the only time we can fast to hear from God.

My decision was a big sacrifice. I *love* television. I spend hours and hours with television. We're tight, and breaking up with it—even if only temporarily—was not an easy decision. That meant no weekly network shows, no Food Network, no Netflix. Nada TV! Aargh!

Knowing how it calls to me like a long-lost friend in moments of fatigue, boredom, and procrastination, I knew if I wanted to be serious about spending more time with Jesus, I had to *cancel* my subscription to Netflix. End it. Be done. No Access. No more British dramas, hilarious sitcoms, or mysterious whodunits.

The first couple days I thought, *What was I thinking? If I was going to fast from something, why didn't I choose something easier—like reading the Bible in its original language or running a marathon or solving world hunger?*

But after a week, I knew the answer. God wants me to

be hungry for him. To have time and a quiet space to hear him. When I long for a Netflix fix (oh, and I do long for it), God is calling me to long for him. Instead of pondering and worrying about how fictitious characters are going to get out of their jam or what's going to happen in the next episode, God wants me to think about how he has rescued me! To lean into his faithfulness for my future.

Instead of *Just one more episode*, I began to have time to read, call a friend, sit reflectively, exercise (well, I hardly ever think that), but you get the idea.

More and more, I began to hear God's whisper traipse across the backyard of my brain. I felt his presence as I read his words in my Bible. I was filled with love and wonder and wisdom.

As Steve Harmon says, "Everyone wants to be transformed, but nobody wants to change." That's why God calls us to fast, so that change will lead us to be transformed.

After I ended the fast, I acknowledged the good that came from it. Without the distraction of television, I was offered a time of self-examination and reflection to consider who God is, what he's done, and how to respond to him.

Have you ever considered going deeper with God by fasting from something that only keeps you distracted? Maybe it's television, or social media, or the news. Whatever it is, it's the golden opportunity to institute a change that could revolutionize your thinking, your spirit, and your life.

Ask God what you can give up to experience his presence in a more powerful way.

Then prepare to be amazed.

# Prayer

O God, I want to know you more.
I want to hear your still, small voice.
I want to see you move in my life
and in the lives of others. Help me
find you in this world that contends
for my every minute and attention.
I want to let go of that which keeps
me distant and questioning. Meet me
in the space I create for you and me.
In Jesus' name, amen.

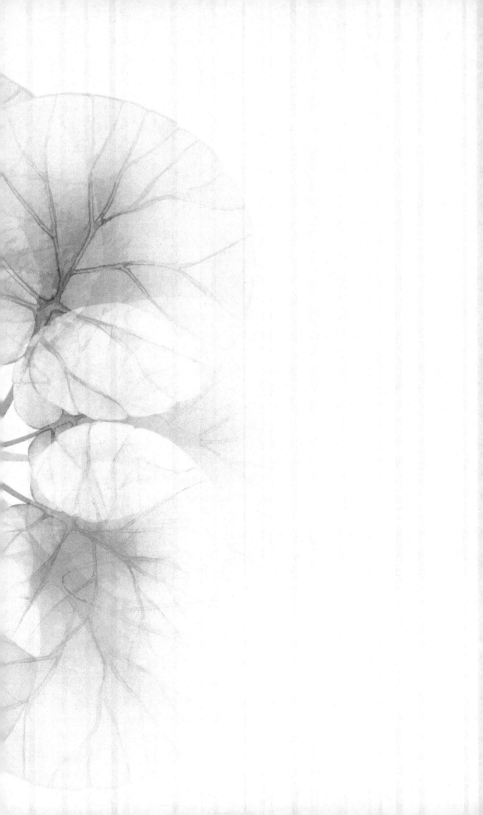

# 12

# THE SECRET TO BEING THANKFUL

Sing and make music from your heart
to the Lord, always giving thanks to
God the Father for everything,
in the name of our Lord Jesus Christ.

—EPHESIANS 5:19–20

*W*hen I learned to drive motorcycles, I discovered very quickly that where you look is where you go! Through the curves, around the obstacles, or into the ditch! The same is true in our everyday lives—it's easy to lose our focus.

If you're anything like me, you can start to concentrate more on what everyone else is doing, decorating, devouring, or delighting in. But comparisons take up the space in our minds and hearts that God is supposed to inhabit.

Instead of being thankful for what I have, too often I can focus on what *she* has, or what *she* does, or what *she* gets, or how *she* looks. I compare home-decorating skills, culinary prowess, the number of Facebook likes she gets, and the size of her dress.

The problem with comparisons is that things are not always what they seem. Comparing *her* Facebook life to *my* real life is never a good plan. No one I know posts pictures of the burned dinner, broken hearts, or binge eating. Comparisons are only good for statisticians.

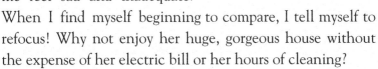

It's my experience that comparing my house with the neighbor's house can make me feel sad and inadequate. When I find myself beginning to compare, I tell myself to refocus! Why not enjoy her huge, gorgeous house without the expense of her electric bill or her hours of cleaning?

Comparing my "Pinterest fail" plate of homemade cookies could make me feel like the worst baker in the potluck group. But when I refocus, I can enjoy the delicacies created by someone with more talent and time to spend in the kitchen!

Comparing the diamond necklace my coworker got from her husband could make me feel that I am sorely lacking in the fine jewelry department. But when I refocus, I recognize that Mr. 4-Ever makes me feel like a diamond every day.

The secret to being thankful is where we place our focus. It's time to let go of comparisons and turn our attention toward being thankful for what God has blessed us with. And it's plenty!

Tell God what you're thankful for. From the grandest gift of your salvation to the minutest of details. You'll be pleasantly surprised by the peace that falls and the joy that will bubble in your heart.

# *Prayer*

Lord, sometimes I get distracted

by what I don't have rather than

being grateful for all that I do have.

I'm never without your presence

or grace or blessings. Thank you,

Father, for being such a good gift giver.

Your gifts are all around me! When

I start to compare myself to others,

refocus my perspective.

Make me ever mindful of what

I can be thankful for. Amen.

# 13

# ABOUT THAT CHALLENGING PERSON IN YOUR LIFE . . .

Truly I tell you,
whatever you did for one of the
least of these brothers and sisters
of mine, you did for me.

—MATTHEW 25:40

*O*ne of my fathers-in-law was a Golden Gloves boxing champion for the army during WWII. After leaving the army, he joined the police force in Milwaukee, Wisconsin. He rode motorcycles year-round in the freezing Wisconsin winters.

"*#^%, yes, it was cold," he'd say. "We'd wrap our legs with newspaper as insulation under our uniforms." He was a strong man with strong opinions and not much of a filter, if you know what I mean.

At least his sweet wife buffered his coarse talk and old-fashioned opinions with graceful scoldings and smiles.

Then his wife died. Suddenly I became the primary caregiver for that cantankerous man!

He moved into our home and went everywhere the kids and I went—grocery stores, swimming pools, restaurants. What he couldn't flirt with, he fought with. He made unfriendly gestures at drivers using their cell phones. He told off-color stories at the dinner table. He woke kids from naps they didn't want to take and gave them treats they weren't supposed to have.

He'd pat me on the backside and say, "Hey, baby, how you doin' today?"

I wondered how long it would be before my head exploded. I would have done just about anything to get rid of him.

But then I found Proverbs 25:21–22: "If your enemy is hungry, give him food to eat; if he is thirsty, give him water to drink. In doing this, you will heap burning coals on his head, and the LORD will reward you."

Right on! Burning coals for him and a reward for me! What's not to like?

I kept taking care of him, but I didn't see any burning-coal consequences for him, and I sensed *no reward* for me.

I felt frustrated—and I let God know about it.

After complaining to God about him for the millionth time, one morning during my quiet time, I found myself staring at another Scripture passage in Matthew 25. Here Jesus is talking to a crowd, and he says, "I was hungry and you gave me something to eat, I was thirsty and you gave me something to drink, I was a stranger and you invited me in, I needed clothes and you clothed me, I was sick and you looked after me" (verses 35–36).

When the crowd asks him when they had done all that, Jesus answers, "Truly I tell you, whatever you did for one of the least of these brothers and sisters of mine, you did for me" (verse 40).

Oh no! I felt awful. Taking care of someone for a reward is much different from caring for people the way Jesus would. The burning coals were falling on *my* head!

I started treating my father-in-law as if Jesus was

following me around taking notes. I took care of him cheerfully. I spoke to him kindly. I served him graciously. I prayed for him continually.

At the end his life, I can tell you he had not changed a lick.

But I had. I had learned patience, hospitality, mercy, kindness. I had learned to love him as Jesus loved him. As is.

Just as Jesus loves me.

So about that challenging person in your life . . . which head are the burning coals falling on?

# *Prayer*

God, I have a difficult person
in my life and I want to treat that
person as you want me to—not
because I relish the idea of heaping
burning coals on their head, but
because I need to treat them
exactly as if I am treating you. Help
me. Give me strength, especially
when it's the most difficult.
In Jesus' name, amen.

# 14

# TRUSTING GOD WHEN LIFE GETS DIFFICULT

Those who know your name

trust in you, for you, LORD,

have never forsaken those

who seek you.

—PSALM 9:10

*I*t was the worst day of Catherine's life. Her daughter was stillborn. Instead of going home from the hospital with a healthy baby, she carried a full diaper bag and an empty baby seat. At home she dealt with the hormones and milk-filled breasts. All the while avoiding a nursery filled with stuffed toys and rocking chairs.

In her grief Catherine was angry. Instead of leaning into God, she turned her back on him, convinced that God had deserted her and was cruel in a way she could not fathom. Her anger turned to depression. Soon she found sleep so elusive, she drank at night to try to help her sleep and slept all day because she was tired and hung over.

She stopped going to church because it hurt too much to see pregnant women and young children. It took almost six months before she could even look to heaven. And when she finally did, she realized that her anger with God wasn't getting her anywhere but deeper into pain. She let go of the offense she had against God, asked for his forgiveness and restoration, and he flooded her brokenness with peace.

That's when the healing finally began. "It took a long time, and I still don't understand why it happened," she said, "but after I surrendered my anger to Jesus, my faith became and continues to grow stronger. I can trust that God has a plan, even if I don't understand it."

We've all been there, haven't we? Wondering how we'll make it through this hardship or that trauma? Wondering why God allows more than we can handle, or why he allows us to go through things that make no sense.

As I look in the Bible, I find dozens of stories about

ordinary people who demonstrate exemplary trust in God
to receive extraordinary
outcomes—particularly
in the toughest times.

One of my favor-
ites is when Joshua was
leading the Israelites in
the charge of Jericho.
They had just celebrated
the miracle of crossing the
raging Jordan River on dry
land. The next obstacle to the
promised land was the walled city of Jericho.

*What's the plan, God?* they must have wondered. *Fire from heaven? Angel armies? A holy earthquake?*

No one would have conceived that the great battle plan to take Jericho was to march around the city once a day for six days, and then seven times on the seventh day and then shout really loudly. But Joshua trusted God, and the whole city collapsed to be plundered.

As Catherine trusted the Lord, she discovered that the same God who led Joshua into the promised land could lead her out of her wilderness too.

Who would ever have guessed that Joseph, the favorite son of Jacob, would end up stripped of his coat of many col-ors, be sold into slavery, be falsely accused of rape, end up in jail to rot—but then rise to rule Egypt and be placed in a strategic role to save his family from famine?

Catherine discovered that the same God who was with Joseph in his captivity could lead her out of her prison too.

Trusting that God is in the business of restoration and redemption takes faith—the kind of faith that grows in the muck of hardship.

Where do you turn when life is hard? What do you do when you pray and don't get the answer you need? How do you find the courage to trust God in the worst of situations? Girlfriend, I don't know what you're facing today, but I do know that God is ready with a plan to redeem and restore you. Lift your eyes to heaven and ask him for the plan.

# Prayer

Lord God Almighty, when life is
out of control, when life is too hard
to handle alone, when circumstances
are beyond my ability to control or
even make sense of, enter in.
I'm inviting you into my chaos and
asking you to be God over me
and my situation. Amen.

# 15

# UNINVITED AND OVERLOOKED

Fix your thoughts on what is true, and
honorable, and right, and pure, and lovely,
and admirable. Think about things that are
excellent and worthy of praise.
Keep putting into practice all you learned
and received from me— everything you
heard from me and saw me doing.
Then the God of peace will be with you.

—PHILIPPIANS 4:8–9 NLT

*I* was hanging out with several friends when they began to chatter away about a party *everyone* had gone to. Everyone except me.

The conversation turned awkward when they realized I hadn't been asked to the festivities my friends were reminiscing about.

I found myself in a similar situation a few days later when I was scanning through my Facebook newsfeed. My smile faded when I saw the beaming faces of friends at another friend's wedding I wasn't invited to attend.

And I dealt with another hurtful situation when a relative died but no one thought to notify me. Tears fell hot as I read the note with the outdated news.

Not included. Not invited. Not remembered.

Have you ever been in that situation? It hurts, doesn't it? How do you handle it?

When it happens to me, I'm tempted to curl up in a fetal position and suck my proverbial thumb till the hurt goes away.

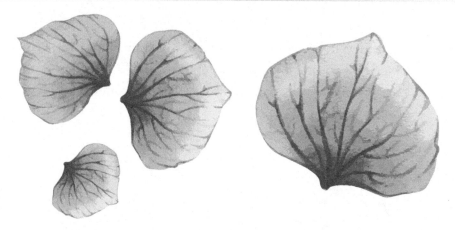

Or I think about ways to get back at them. Maybe I could pretend it doesn't bother me and post my own fun pictures of a recent exploit. Or I could retaliate and blast off a nasty text or a blistering email. Or I could run—but where would I go to outrun the hurt?

It's inevitable that at some point in our lives, we will get hurt, overlooked, forgotten, not invited. Those are the times especially when God opens his arms to us and invites us to run to him. As the psalmist reminds us: "The LORD is close to the brokenhearted and saves those who are crushed in spirit" (Psalm 34:18).

When we are feeling left out, overlooked, forgotten, we can know that in fact, we aren't. We belong to the One who will never leave us or forsake us. That One has our names on his heart. And we are always invited into his presence.

It's in the presence of God that we can find the grace, humility, and courage to forgive and extend our heart to those who didn't invite us, include us, or remember us.

So the next time hurt happens, run to God. Cry out to

him and wait for his peace to fall. Let the Holy Spirit whisper to you that you are loved and accepted by the One who made you, that you are always included, never alone, and certainly never forgotten.

# Prayer

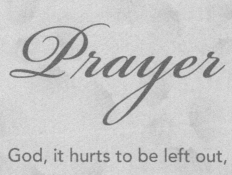

God, it hurts to be left out,

overlooked, not included.

Be the caulk that fills in the

cracks of my broken heart.

Remind me that I can trust

you to always love me,

celebrate me, invite me.

Amen.

# 16

# GOD'S MYSTERIOUS ANSWERS TO PRAYER

A man's heart
plans his way,
but the LORD directs
his steps.

PROVERBS 16:9 NKJV

From my home office, I could hear the racket. Loud, clunking, arrhythmic noises were coming from something big and mechanical. At first, I thought the washing machine was out of balance and trying to walk out of the basement again, but I quickly discovered my central air conditioning unit was the source of the noise.

No air conditioning . . . and it was ninety degrees outside, with a lot more summer on the calendar. I shut down the unit and called the repair man. His assessment?

"Call the sales office. You need a new one," he told me.

"There's no way to fix this one?"

"Lady," he said, "this unit is twenty-two years old. It's served you well. Let it die in peace."

"Well, can you estimate what it will cost to replace?"

Without a moment of hesitation, he said, "I'd guess close to $3,000."

I nearly fainted—and not from the heat! I didn't have an extra $3,000 lying around waiting to be spent on a new air conditioner. I'd just have to limp along without it.

But the next day was another blinger! Hot and humid. I tried to coax the air conditioner to work, if even for a little while. "Come on, please cool the air," I begged it.

It sputtered for a minute or two and then started making the clunking noise again.

This was war! I went outside, laid my hands on that contraption, and prayed for it to come back to life. "Lord, nothing is impossible for you," I said. "I believe you can easily restore this machine. But if this machine is not to be resurrected, then I pray for a money miracle. Provide an unexpected windfall or provide unexpected benevolence to pay for a new air conditioner. In Jesus' name I pray and thank you in advance. Amen."

I went back in the house and waited. And that night my prayer was answered—only, not in the way you'd expect or even the way I prayed. The temperature outside fell into the forties! I opened the windows and let the cool air displace the heat.

The next morning the house was so cold, I had to dig out a sweater to put on. I giggled with delight at God's creative solution.

I had come up with a plan and presented my suggestion to God. I even gave him alternatives in case he needed choices. He came up with an answer I never conceived of.

Though I didn't know how long those unseasonably cool days and nights would last, they had been a sign from God that he saw me, he heard me, he was concerned for me, and he was working on my behalf.

I am all about big, bold, specific prayers, but I know I have to let God decide how and when to answer them. My job is to keep pressing in for more as I wait for him to respond. Through it all, God was teaching me a new lesson about growing my faith—that the end of my resources is just the beginning of God's.

He creates and solves and delivers in ways we couldn't ask or even dream of. His storehouses are stocked beyond our imagination. Our job is to pray and trust. God will determine how and when to deliver.

# Prayer

God, when I get so worried
about things, help me to
remember that you have all
the solutions to all my issues
and problems. Big dilemmas
for me are nothing for you.
Remind me that nothing
is impossible for you.

Amen.

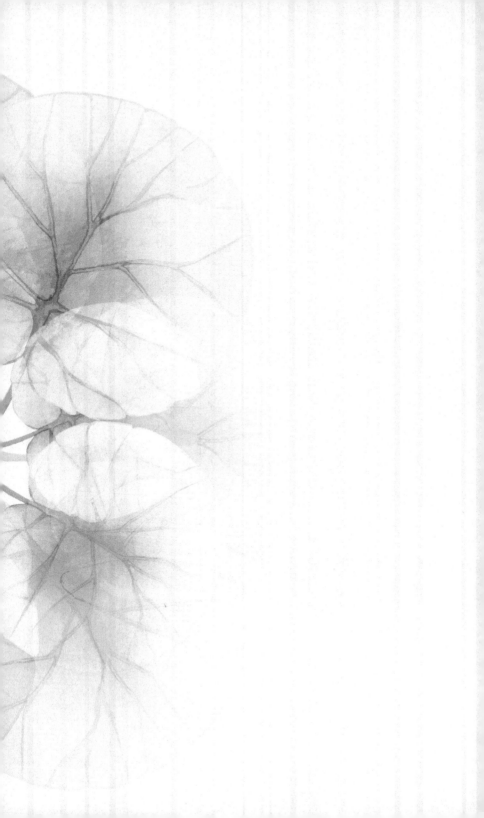

# 17

## MAKING THE CONNECTION

❧

I remain confident of this:
I will see the goodness of the LORD
in the land of the living.
Wait for the LORD;
be strong and take heart
and wait for the LORD.

—PSALM 27:13–14

*L*ast summer Dave and I went to a conference in Toronto, Canada. We were *together* for six days—joined at the hip! In the car. In the hotel room. At the conference. Eating. Sleeping. Driving. Learning. Ministering . . . together!

On our first morning back at home, while I was having my quiet time, Dave came in and smiled. "Good morning! Let me get my coffee and sit next to you. We haven't spent any down time together for a while."

Had he not remembered the previous week in which that was *all* we did? Honestly, at first I thought, *Argh, I do not have time for a meandering conversation or meaningful togetherness right now! I have to unpack, do laundry, take a friend in for a colonoscopy, pick up something for dinner, write my Bible study leaders to see how they are doing, finish my blog, and make a dessert for tomorrow night! I do not have any more time for* you!

Fortunately, the Holy Spirit helped me see things from his perspective. Dave could have been sick of me because he couldn't get away from me! Instead, he chose to pursue more time with me to connect—even though he had a lot of things on his own to-do list.

At the heart of any relationship is the time spent together when it's accessible, not just when it's convenient. It's about spending time working out solutions to problems and spending time just being, just talking, and just enjoying each other's company. For any relationship to work, we have to put in the time.

Whether we are Velcroed to kids all day, swamped by

coworkers' questions, or connected at
the hip to our hubbies, the time
we invest in our relationships is
what makes them work.

That applies to our rela-
tionship with God as well.
He wants us to spend time
with him when it's accessible, not just convenient. And
he's *always* accessible. There
is no such thing as too much
togetherness with God.

For a deeper connection with
God, set aside a time most days (if not all)
to read his Word. It will reveal his love for you, and his
character, and will speak to your situation. Even when it
feels inconvenient, it's time well spent. You don't have to
read for an hour; you can do a little bit most days. Read a
chapter a day. Ask Siri or another device to read you a story
from the Old Testament while you do your makeup or drive
to work. Don't look at this reading (or listening) as a chore.
Think of it as a date to look forward to.

Spending time in God's Word and in prayer assures
you of his love and acceptance. It fortifies your faith in his
ability and willingness to intervene on your behalf. It estab-
lishes you as worthy and significant.

What are you reading these days to strengthen your
relationship with your Creator?

I'm in Exodus, reading about Moses and the courage he

mustered to serve God as he led the Hebrews out of Egypt. As I'm reading, I'm hearing God whisper to me that, as I follow him, he will equip me for the tasks he calls me to.

Are you giving him the time of day? Are you quiet long enough to hear his still, small voice whispering to you? Does he feel close and affirming or distant and aloof? He wants a connected togetherness with you.

# Prayer

Father, I want to know you better.

I want to believe more.

I want to be able to trust you fully.

Put a "want to" in me

to spend time with you

as often as I can.

In Jesus' name, amen.

# 18

# CHANGE IS GOOD

No temptation [trial or change]
has overtaken you except something
common to mankind;
and God is faithful, so He will not allow
you to be tempted beyond
what you are able, but with
the temptation will provide the way
of escape also, so that you will
be able to endure it.

—1 CORINTHIANS 10:13 NASB

*I*n my quiet time this morning, I realized I was sitting on a twenty-five-year-old couch, looking at faux-finish painted walls that were all the rage about twenty-five years ago, wearing a robe that is, you guessed it, almost twenty-five years old.

I do not like change—even if it's my idea! But just because I hate change does not mean it doesn't happen anyway.

Things break and wear out. Children grow up and move away. Friends take on new interests and invite us to join them or leave us behind. Opportunities evolve and disintegrate. Change is inevitable.

Change serves God's purpose: it is how he gets our attention and grows our faith in him. Without change, we can get stuck in patterns and habits that become familiar, self-reliant, and possibly destructive.

In Exodus 9, God commanded the shepherd Moses, a man with a speech impediment, to return to Egypt, a land he'd fled to avoid prosecution for murder, to talk Pharaoh into freeing millions of slaves.

In Judges 7, Gideon—a farmer with no military experience—was interrupted from his wheat threshing to go fight several hundred thousand Midianites with only three hundred men, each armed with a torch, a trumpet, and a pitcher!

Change engages our trust. There is a *big* difference between believing God *is* and trusting God *will* provide the support, the words, the victory, the healing, or the way through change on time and in time!

Over the years, Holy Spirit has whispered, *Trust me*, more times than I can count. But I counter with, *What if I can't do this thing you're asking of me?*

See, I know God loves and cares about me. I know nothing is impossible for him. I know that all the promises in the Bible are as true today as when they were written. But I often have a disconnect. I believe that even though God *can* do all things, there is a distinct possibility he might not.

When faced with contentious relationships, an ugly diagnosis, rebellious children, financial crises, disorder or chaos of any kind, the temptation is to falter—not in our belief of *who God is* but in our distrust of *what he'll do*. When it gets right down to it, we don't trust that God will make things turn out the way *we* want them to.

That's why change is so important: it flexes our trust muscles.

So the next time the potential for change shows up at our doorstep, rather than shrink back from it, let's do our best to embrace it, knowing that God is ready to do something through it to speak to our hearts and challenge our faith to new levels.

If it's scary, that's okay. That's when we need to review our history and remind ourselves of all the things that have not killed us or resulted in the end of a relationship or financial ruin or a health crisis, that not only came to pass, but forti-fied our faith in God.

Change is difficult, of that there is no doubt. But know-ing God uses it to draw us closer and make us stronger can help us face it, trusting him to get us through.

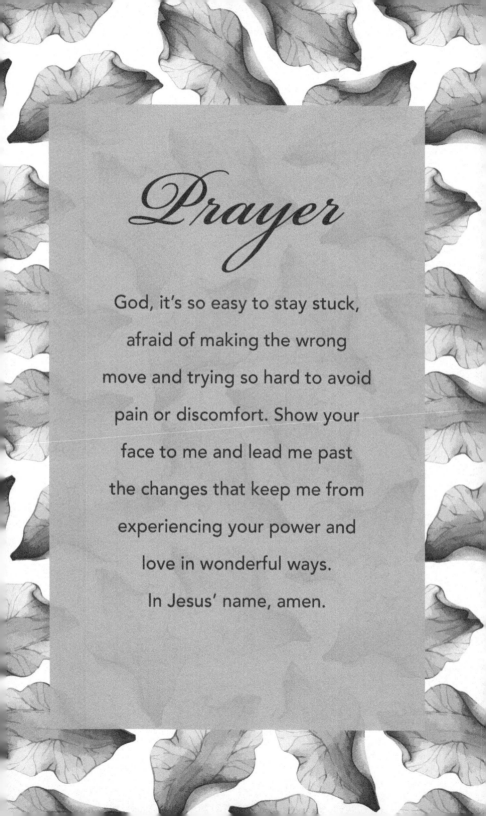

# Prayer

God, it's so easy to stay stuck,
afraid of making the wrong
move and trying so hard to avoid
pain or discomfort. Show your
face to me and lead me past
the changes that keep me from
experiencing your power and
love in wonderful ways.
In Jesus' name, amen.

# 19

# APPROACH WITH CAUTION TO AVOID REPROACH!

As God's chosen people,
holy and dearly loved,
clothe yourselves with compassion,
kindness, humility, gentleness
and patience.

—COLOSSIANS 3:12

*I*t all started when I lost my car keys. Also, my new barrettes (still in the package), two socks (not a pair), and ultimately my temper. It wasn't a world-class snit; it was a slow-burning, internal sizzle.

I was snippy because I don't lose things. I just don't. I'm organized. I'm tidy. I put things away. It's fair to say I'm even a little arrogant about my superior system for organized tidiness. There is a place for everything, and everything should be in its place! But this day I could not find my things.

*Where are my keys? Ugh.*

After I turned the house upside down looking, I decided to pray. I had come to the end of myself. My best organizing and retrieval system had failed me. My prayer was bold! "God, *where are my keys?*" I demanded of heaven.

By that point, my pride had gone into overdrive, and I didn't care as much about finding my keys as I did about not wanting to admit that I'd lost them. As the day wore on without any results or answers, I started grumbling. And worrying.

*Am I losing my mind?* Alzheimer's runs in my family. *Is this how it starts?* I mentally tested myself. I could remember the names and birthdates of my children and all my husbands. *Probably not Alzheimer's.*

Finally, I asked Dave, Mr. 4-Ever, if he would help me.

"Sure," he said good naturedly, completely ignoring my testiness. Within minutes he produced my keys.

"What? How did . . . Where were they?" I asked incredulously.

"In your purse."

"But I looked in my purse!"

"Well," he said, "I asked God where your keys were, and he said to look in your purse, so I did, and there they were."

Here's the lesson I quickly learned: when we storm heaven's gates, we need to make sure our motives are pure.

I was so bent on proving my system of organizing that my pride got in the way of a solution. I'd been so busy fussing, squawking, grumbling, and worrying that I could hardly think, much less go to the Lord humbly or quietly enough to hear God's still, small voice.

Friend, I still don't know where the new barrettes and socks are, but my keys and my calm were quickly restored.

How about you? Do you get yourself into such a snit that you can't hear from God? When you pray for answers, for solutions, for direction, for guidance, do you approach boldly but with humility?

When we've worked ourselves into a snit, that's the time to calm down, take a breath, ask for what we need, then listen intently. God has all the answers we need. He wants us to come humbly and ask.

# Prayer

God, do I amuse you with my

efforts to try to make my life work

without considering you?

Do I hurt you when I'm so rattled

that I can't hear you? I know that

your systems are dependable.

I know that your love will always

redeem. Thank you for the

reminder and the fresh start

as often as I need it. Amen.

# 20

# BREAKING FREE
# FROM THE
# TRAP OF SIN

Submit yourselves, then, to God. Resist
the devil,
and he will flee from you.

—JAMES 4:7

*T*his past weekend I almost dug brownies out of the garbage can. The willpower I had to toss them in the trash at 6:00 p.m. was completely gone at 10:30 p.m., and I wanted those brownies in the worst way. Who cares that I'd have to rummage through the garbage can outside with a flashlight? So what if I had to scrape a few coffee grounds off of them?

If Mr. 4-Ever hadn't caught me in the act, I'm sure I would have written this devotion with fingers covered in gooey chocolate, feeling awful and disgusted with myself and thinking, *I never meant for this to happen.*

Scrounging gross brownies from a garbage can isn't that big an aberration, but we can get caught up in things that definitely are, things we never dreamed would hook us and can have lasting and devastating effects. Prescription drugs. Alcohol. Lies and deceptions. Overspending and debt. Codependency. Pornography. Abusive relationships.

Carolyn got caught up in bad decisions and regret. When I met with her, she couldn't even look at me. Finally, she confessed, "I'm having an affair with a married man. We met at work, and over the course of conversation, cocktails, and compliments, I found myself taken in by him. It felt nice to be noticed. Not just for the way I look but for my brain and my ideas. Now here I am, three years into a relationship with a man who will never divorce his wife. My whole life has become about hiding the truth from my family and friends, swallowing the pain and guilt, and pretending everything is great. I've tried to break it off, but I keep going back."

I stared at her. Why would a beautiful, educated woman allow herself to be used like this?

*Because sin is delicious.* Sin wraps itself in what looks harmless or helpful or inviting, like the man who is kind to us on a rough day. Or the prescription that numbs the pain. Or the images on the computer screen that take us from real life. Or the glass of wine with dinner that turns into three or four.

Sin sneaks in and tastes so good.

Pretty soon, we're back for another nibble and another and another. Before we know it, all we can think about is the sensation of it. But the fear of being found out, rejected, judged, escalates. Pretty soon, we feel trapped in the guilt and shame.

That's the way Carolyn felt. And that trapped feeling made her believe the big lie that she had no way out.

We worked together until she broke free of the relationship and received restoration from God. It was tough, but the joy and peace that came out of it was the reward of confessing and breaking free.

Maybe you're feeling trapped right now, and you don't see a way out. Maybe you've even been a Christian for years, but you still struggle with being trapped. Sweet friend, Jesus didn't just die for the little sins you can live with. He didn't just die for the sins you can manage to forgive yourself for. Jesus died for the huge, stinky atrocities that make you feel so rotten you believe you deserve whatever trap you find yourself in.

It's time to break free.

Confess the sin or addiction or behavior specifically (1 John 1:9), tell God you're done with it (Acts 3:19), ask him to take away the urge and blockade the path to another nibble (2 Corinthians 5:17), and then receive God's forgiveness (John 3:16–17).

Jesus, our crucified Savior, has risen victorious over sin and death. The same power that raised Jesus from the dead lives in you. Believe he extends that gift to you today. Receive it for yourself and spring the trap open for good.

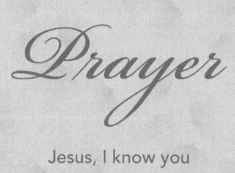

# Prayer

Jesus, I know you

did not die so I would live

condemned in this world.

Forgive me. Lead me to freedom.

I need you. I need help.

I want a different life than this.

Amen.

# 21

## DREAM BIG!

Do not despise
these small beginnings,
for the LORD rejoices
to see the work begin.

—ZECHARIAH 4:10 NLT

*I* spend a lot of my days doing ordinary stuff. Boring stuff. Familiar stuff.

I clean bathrooms. I wash clothes. I fix meals.

Sometimes it really gets to me, you know? I have big dreams of doing important things! As a speaker and writer, I dream of seeing thousands surrender to Jesus. I have big dreams of women breaking free of stinkin' thinkin'. I have big dreams of infusing hope to the bowed down.

But sometimes those big dreams get lost in the day-to-day drudgery of life.

You too, right?

Does that happen to your big dreams, big goals, big plans? I'm not talking so much about your bucket list. I'm wondering about the big call on your life. The thing that makes you hopping mad or brings you to tears or makes your heart beat faster when you think and talk about it.

You have a vision to change the world, or at least your corner of it, but you get interrupted by unexpected pregnancies, and babies who need changing, and toddlers who need training, and teens who need redirection, and your neighbor whose car needs a jump, and your house that needs cleaning, and your marriage that needs a spark of romance. And your dream/goal/project sits dormant.

We lose momentum when we encounter resistance. We begin to complain and grumble. We falter when the tasks become hard or mundane. Fear of failure, rejection, and judgment seizes us and threatens to derail us.

That's when we need to dig back in and start pursuing our goal again. There's a little verse in Zechariah 4:10 that tells us not to despise small beginnings, because God celebrates when he sees us beginning the work. Beginning is just as important as accomplishing. Even if it's slow and filled with interruptions, God wants us to get to work on that dream, goal, or plan.

Do you need to be reignited?

Don't be discouraged by the distractions of life, the naysayers, the slow starts, or the interruptions of your everyday. If you got derailed or detained or distracted or even temporarily disinterested, don't despair. Keep dreaming big dreams! Take as many fresh starts as you need.

Small beginnings lead to big things. Your child raised well. Your business flourishing. Your book completed. Your home renovated. Your church revived.

There is no shame in starting again . . . and again. Keep giving yourself fresh starts until you have accomplished that big dream, goal, or plan God has given you and created you for.

What's your big dream to change your corner of the world?

# Prayer

God, sometimes I can become
so frustrated because I have big
dreams but I feel like I'm stuck in the
mundane routines of everyday life
that keep me from pursuing them.
Thank you for reminding me that
small beginnings are nothing to be
ashamed of, and that you rejoice in
the work I start. Help me start—
and keep pursuing—even if it's in
small steps along the way. Amen.

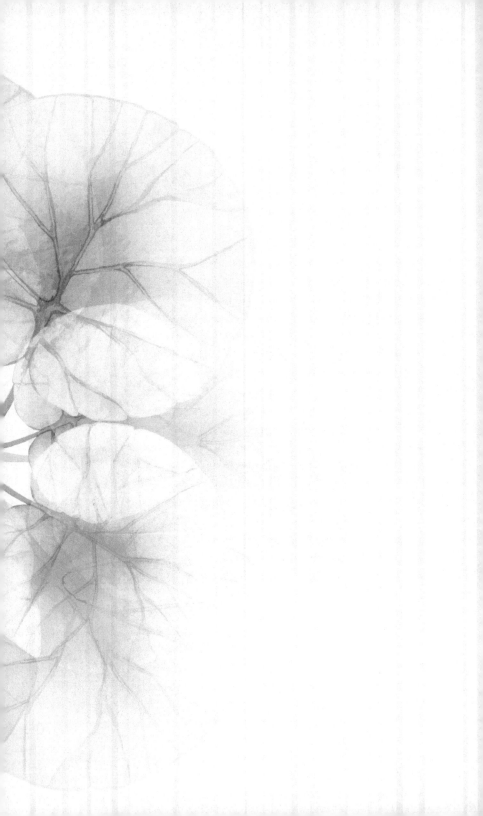

# 22

# DON'T LET BITTER ROOTS GROW

See to it that no one falls
short of the grace of God and
that no bitter root grows up
to cause trouble and defile many.

—HEBREWS 12:15

One Christmas, as usual, I texted both my grown boys and reminded them to make sure they had Christmas cards in the mail to their grandparents. By implication, I figured they would recognize it as a subtle reminder to send one to me too. If not a gift, at least a card. After all, I gave them life!

Well. Christmas came and went and nothing from my youngest. New Year's passed and nada from him. By mid-January, bitterness and hurt was taking root, and I knew I'd have to talk to him.

When he called, asking how I was, I told him. "I'm kinda down. Someone hurt my feelings."

"Aww, that stinks, Mom. What happened?"

"You didn't send me a Christmas card."

Immediately, he said, "Oh, Mom, I'm so sorry. It just got away from me. Do you want me to still send you one?"

Without any hesitation, I said, "Yes. Yes, I do."

The next week, I got a lovely non-Christmas card. Since it was mid-January, he had no choice but to improvise. The card had butterflies and blossoms on the front and a beautiful sentiment inside, that said, "Mom, sorry I didn't get this to you sooner. I love you so much and am very glad I'm your son. You're the best mom in the world! Love you lots, Eli."

One quick, awkward conversation cut down a bitter root and restored the peace between us.

When little kids fight, they flare, they pout, they tattle, and they make up. It's over! As we get older and get into conflicts, we tend to foster bitterness, hold on to grudges, and plot retaliation.

That is exactly the opposite of God's desire for us. He created us to live in harmony with him and with others. Hebrews 12:14–15 specifically says, "*Work* at living in peace with everyone, and *work* at living a holy life, for those who are not holy will not see the Lord. Look after each other so that none of you fails to receive the grace of God. Watch out that no poisonous root of bitterness grows up to trouble you, corrupting many" (NLT, emphasis added).

That's right, we have to work at living in peace with everyone because we each have opinions and systems we believe are the correct ones. We all have soft spots and past hurts that we want to protect. When we bump into someone who triggers us, it's super easy for an offense to grow, bitterness to take root, and our version of justice to be meted out.

The right, but hard, thing to do when an offense is blossoming or when bitterness has taken root is to have a conversation with the person you're honked at. If you get used to having awkward conversations about little things, you'll be practiced and brave enough to have a hard conversation when a bigger offense develops.

Friend, God knew conflict was going to happen to all of us, so he provided a way of restoring peace and harmony in our hearts and relationships. In Matthew 18:15, the plan is clearly laid out: "If your brother or sister sins [offends], go and point out their fault [what has you so upset], just between the two of you. If they listen to you, you have won them over."

The Message version says, "If a fellow believer hurts you, go and tell him—work it out between the two of you. If he listens, you've made a friend."

What you should not do is solicit the opinion of forty-five other people in hopes of recognition and affirmation of the offense. Don't post the offense on Facebook or send an angry text. Call or sit down with the person and have the conversation so peace can prevail. Explain what happened to upset you, and come to an agreement to resolve the conflict.

Whom do you need to be at peace with? Is there a hard conversation you've been putting off? May today be the day for your peace to be restored.

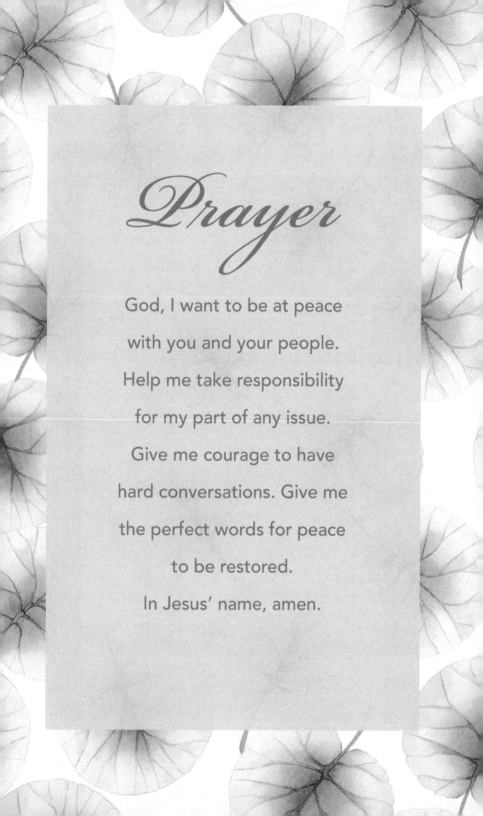

# *Prayer*

God, I want to be at peace

with you and your people.

Help me take responsibility

for my part of any issue.

Give me courage to have

hard conversations. Give me

the perfect words for peace

to be restored.

In Jesus' name, amen.

# 23

# COUNT IT ALL JOY?

Consider it pure joy, my brothers
and sisters, whenever you face trials of
many kinds, because you know that the
testing of your faith
produces perseverance.

—JAMES 1:2–3

*M*r. 4-Ever and I had been in the car for five minutes of a twelve-hour trip when a car pulled into our path and Dave swerved to save our lives. Unfortunately, I was drinking a large bottle of Frappuccino when he made his heroic maneuver, and I spilled half the cold, sticky, sugary drink down my front. It splashed into my hair, dripped off my necklace, and soaked my top down to my bra!

Count it all joy?

Earlier that week, on a trip to Florida, I felt something hard in a mouthful of pudding. When my tongue kicked the hard thing out, it was the crown from my front tooth! I was 1,700 miles from my dentist with a scheduled speaking event the next day.

Count it all joy?

The same week, an email from the publisher started with, "I'm sorry to tell you that the truck carrying five thousand of your *The Widow Wore Pink* books to the distribution center caught on fire and *all* of them burned."

Count it all joy?

Girlfriend! Do you have days, weeks, or seasons like this? What would you do if you lost a tooth, had a fire, and experienced a wardrobe malfunction all in the same week?

Stuff happens. And when it does, God's Word says to count it all joy. But how? How do you count it all joy when what you really want to do is pitch a hissy?

*Be thankful!*

Either after the hissy fit (or preferably before), be thankful. As it says in 1 Thessalonians 5:18, "Give thanks in all circumstances; for this is God's will for you in Christ Jesus."

Find what is good in the situation and be thankful. For me, I was grateful that my computer wasn't in my lap to get drenched with Frappuccino goodness; a local dentist I found on Google recemented my fang back in place; and my books can be reprinted, and insurance covered the loss.

Choose *not* to grumble or complain. The damage is done. Grumbling and complaining do nothing to resolve the problem. Now is the time to persevere, regroup, and choose the best course of action to restore or correct the situation. Assess the damage and ask God for wisdom to proceed.

*Remember, God is on the throne.* No one is exempt from bad stuff happening to them, but God is able to redeem, replace, avenge, and reconcile anything and everything, because our God reigns. As our faith grows and we trust God to lead us through, he will mature us to make us more and more like Jesus.

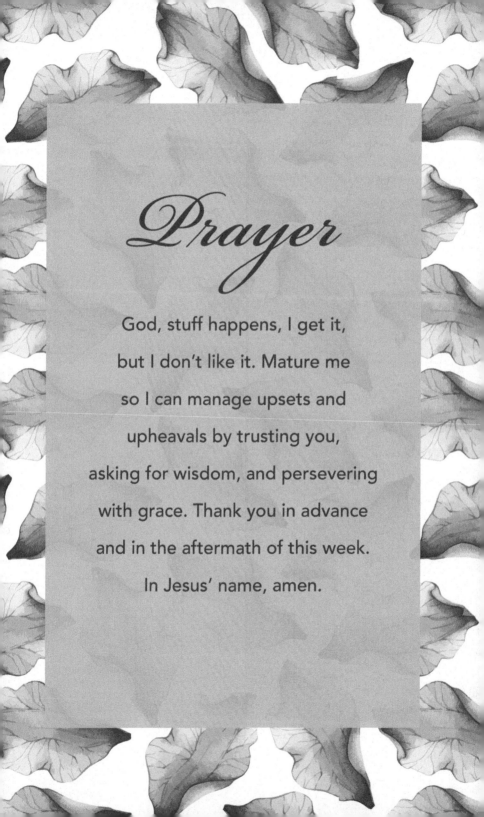

# Prayer

God, stuff happens, I get it,
but I don't like it. Mature me
so I can manage upsets and
upheavals by trusting you,
asking for wisdom, and persevering
with grace. Thank you in advance
and in the aftermath of this week.
In Jesus' name, amen.

# 24

# HAVING A MOMENT

I have learned the secret of being
content in any and every situation,
whether well fed or hungry,
whether living in plenty or in want.
I can do all this through him
who gives me strength.

—PHILIPPINES 4:12–13

*Y*ou ever have a "moment"? Everything is just "fine," and then something hits you sideways and you have a *moment*. Maybe you had a Facebook moment when you saw that you weren't included in a party or conversation or outing. Maybe you had a home-improvement moment as you watched all the options HGTV had to offer. Maybe you had a Pinterest moment when you tried your best to recreate the image on your computer screen and it was an unrecognizable failure.

Maybe you had a moment with your kids, your boss, your husband, your scale, or your mirror . . . and the *moment* dissolved your contentment.

My moment came at the tax guy's office. As he looked over all my documents, his mouth tightened into a disapproving grimace. "Robyn, I know this God thing is important to you, but I have to tell you that at your age, you should be thinking about your future. You need to get a real job."

Ugh.

I explained how faithful God continues to be and how, even though the numbers may not show it, I am experiencing his peace and pleasure as I partner with him to proclaim Jesus' name and teach the Bible from coast to coast.

He shook his head, seeing that his advice was falling on deaf ears.

What I'd told him was true, but as I left his office, my contentment asked my confidence for a date and they took off for parts unknown. The evil twins, discouragement and dissatisfaction, moved in to take their place.

I saw my world through their viewfinder. *My car makes funny sounds. My house needs updating. My bank account isn't multiplying, but my weight and wrinkles sure are!*

I had to wrangle my contentment back in place.

The first thing I did was make a list of one hundred things I had to be thankful for. One hundred things! When I consider all I have, the things I don't have diminish in necessity.

Next, I realized I'd lost my contentment because *the tax guy* thought I should be doing better, not because I didn't have what I needed. Many of us lose our contentment not because *we* aren't doing well but because others are doing better, and the comparison kills our contentment. I chose not to relinquish my contentment and peace by comparing my situation to what Tax Guy projected as successful or enough.

Finally, I reframed the story in my mind and heart. I looked at what was going right or moderately well or mostly okay and dwelt on that. What you focus on grows! (I should have that tattooed on my forehead so I see it every time I look in the mirror.)

So what if I didn't speak in arenas or make a million dollars? I get to speak at dozens of events annually, encouraging thousands to trust Jesus.

Being content doesn't mean settling for less than God

has for you. It doesn't mean tolerating sin or abuse toward you. If change for the better is within your grasp, go for it! Contend for more! But if you're where you're supposed to be, doing what you're supposed to do, be content where God has you.

What steals your contentment? What can you do today to get it back?

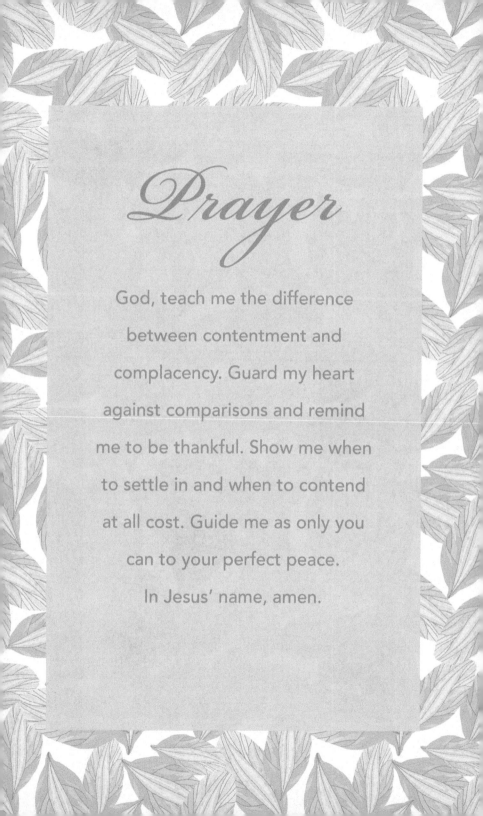

# Prayer

God, teach me the difference

between contentment and

complacency. Guard my heart

against comparisons and remind

me to be thankful. Show me when

to settle in and when to contend

at all cost. Guide me as only you

can to your perfect peace.

In Jesus' name, amen.

# 25

# THE NUDGE

Each of you should use
whatever gift you have received
to serve others, as faithful stewards
of God's grace in its various forms.

—1 PETER 4:10

*I* was waiting at a diner for a girlfriend when I spotted a young man, maybe seventeen years old, staring at a glass of water on the table in front of him. More than giving him a cursory glance, I was compelled to pay attention to him. As I watched him, I distinctly thought, *Buy his meal.* But I stalled.

I didn't want to embarrass him or grandstand. I moved so he wasn't in my line of sight, but the thought to buy his meal persisted. And still I resisted.

You are probably shaking your head right now. How obvious, right? God was speaking! I know, I know. I see it now too, but hindsight has no fear.

The young man left before I took action.

I missed it. I maybe could have made that young man feel like someone cared. That he was seen and that he was loved. But I missed it.

We've all ignored it. That little nudge from the Holy Spirit to go, or do, or say, or help. The nudge is so subtle, it's easy to dismiss as unimportant . . . or ignore if it's inconvenient . . . or disregard if it creates an awkward moment.

When have you missed it? Maybe it was the homeless guy on the side of the road. You were nudged to give a little money, but you talked yourself out of it, because, well, ugh, he'd probably just use it for liquor anyway. Or maybe you got the nudge to check in on a friend, but you were really busy, and she's such a talker, so you told yourself you'd call later.

We've all missed it—the opportunity to love like Jesus loves and do as Jesus did. We get scared or worried about how it will look or what it will cost, and we miss the opportunity.

But when you look back, you feel regret. You wonder, *Why didn't I go or say or do or help?*

Here's the good news: You will undoubtedly get another chance to love as Jesus does and do as Jesus did. Next time, don't make it harder than it needs to be. God equips those he calls to do what he asks—or nudges—us to do.

There is a medical term I learned from my nursing friend. *Potentiate.* Potentiate is when two drugs are taken together and one of them intensifies or accelerates or enhances the effectiveness of the other drug. A spiritual application is that the God-given gift or talent or experience or resource you already have potentiates the love of God to others.

God wants to demonstrate his love to all his people. What did he put in you to potentiate that love?

Are you a woman of prayer? Do you pray without hesitation and with full conviction that you have the ear of God?

Are you a teacher? Can you teach others to cook, or sew, or pray, or balance a checkbook, or read the Bible?

Are you a good listener?

Do you look a talker in the eye and resist the urge to check your phone or look over their shoulder for a more interesting person?

Are you an encourager?

Most women are encouragers, but maybe you take it to

the next level. Do you send cards just because? Are you a master of catching people doing something right and pointing it out?

You may not be able to fix, save, serve, or support everyone, but you can love like Jesus loves, and you can act on the nudge with the gifts, talents, life experiences, and resources you have. And when you do, you'll be blessed with no regret.

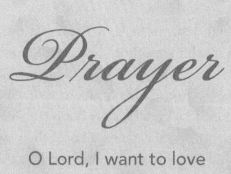

## Prayer

O Lord, I want to love

as Jesus loves and do as

Jesus did. Help me be tuned in

and brave. Make your nudge

obvious, and then give me

the courage to take action.

In Jesus' name, amen.

# ABOUT
# THE AUTHOR

*R*obyn Dykstra is a national Christian speaker, best-selling author, and professional speaking coach. For decades, she has helped thousands of women on their journey to trust God and follow Jesus. She shares her transformation story from Playboy Bunny to Bible teacher at conferences, retreats, and camps all over the United States.

Robyn and Mr. 4-Ever (her husband, aka Dave) are in full-time speaking ministry and are sold-out lovers of God and his Word. Their favorite place to be is on the road proclaiming Jesus, which is a good thing, because they typically speak at forty in-person events annually.

Home for Robyn and Dave is a farmhouse built in 1885 on the outskirts of Grand Rapids, Michigan, where they raised two smart stud-muffins who call and visit their mom often.

For more information about Robyn or her speaking, visit www.robyndykstra.com. Click on events to inquire about having Robyn speak to your women.

If you enjoyed this book from Robyn's Seeds of Inspiration series, check out her other two books in the series. Or get more stories like these at www.robyndykstra.com/blog.

# IF YOU LIKE ROBYN ON THE PAGE YOU'LL LOVE HER ON THE STAGE!

## Invite Robyn to Speak at Your Church:
### ⊕ robyndykstra.com

- ✷ 25 Years Platform Experience
- ✷ Led Thousands to Their Next Step with Jesus
- ✷ 30 Years Bible Teaching Experience

## Featured on:

# GET THE SERIES

**GROWING**
YOUR FAITH

**NURTURING**
YOUR FAITH

**FLOURISHING**
IN YOUR FAITH

robyndykstra.com

Made in the USA
Coppell, TX
12 April 2022

76224058R00090